We Need Bags!

Written by Gill Budgell

Illustrated by Aleksandar Zolotic

RISING STARS

We need lots of bags!
We need book bags for school.

strap

flap

We need bags for shopping

I bring a shopping bag with me.

Food comes in bags.

pet food

crisps

mushrooms

We need bags for sports kits.

zip

pockets

drink

I need a bag for my swimming kit.

plastic

This bag can get wet.

We need lots of bags for a camping trip!

tent bag

peg bag

Things on bags can be fun.

I clip keyrings to my rucksack!

light

Things in bags can be fun.

party bag

gift bag

Talk about the book

Ask your child these questions:

1 Name three bags that were used at school.

2 Which bag could get wet?

3 Why are so many bags needed on a camping trip?

4 Which bag had things clipped on to it?

5 How many different bags can you find at home?

6 Do you have a favourite bag? What does it look like?